SINGLE STEPS

Finding You Before Seeing You

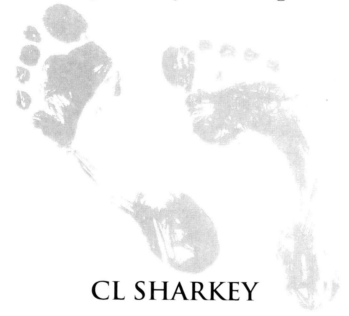

CL SHARKEY

Copyright © 2016 by CL Sharkey

Single Steps
Finding You Before Seeing You
by CL Sharkey

Author photo by Candy's Photography

Printed in the United States of America.

ISBN 9781498489973

All rights reserved solely by the author. The author guarantees all contents are original and do not infringe upon the legal rights of any other person or work. No part of this book may be reproduced in any form without the permission of the author. The views expressed in this book are not necessarily those of the publisher.

Scripture quotations taken from the King James Version (KJV) – *public domain*.

Edited by Xulon Press.

www.xulonpress.com

To all my PUSHERS, I dedicate this work to you for keeping me in step.

&

Harold Oliver Norton for teaching me not to chop the questions but to ASK God.

Table of Contents

WHY? 9

My Story 11

Unplug. 19

Not Comparing Yourself 27

Love Responding to Love 41

Whyfacome? 59

Rise 65

WHY?

"For I reckon that the sufferings of this present time are not worthy to be compared with the glory which shall be revealed in us." Romans 8:18 (KJV)

This verse of Scripture is my foundational scripture because I never understood why things would happen to me or what purpose my life had. My life to me was a series of rejections and mishaps, a life of looking for what was never displayed or given to me. I didn't know what life was supposed to be as a kid; I saw so much stuff, and all kind of things happened. Things that would jack me up for periods in my life and make me wonder, "Why am I here?" I know this may sound like something you've heard before, but keep reading. It's the steps that I took on my journey to help someone else, to be compared to the glory that shall be revealed in us. My trial-and-error life has formed steps to walk up out of the "basement" life with that basement mentality to instead live in the glory that God is revealing and has revealed.

It is my prayer that someone will step up and find out what God has for them, and that you will not compare your present sufferings to the glory that shall be revealed in us. Remember that what's coming out of your sufferings will open doors for others to come out into the glory of God.

MY STORY

Unplug means to take something out of the sockets, to disconnect from the power source. We keep things plugged up to the source of power as a security blanket to keep us in power. We leave it charged, thinking we are in control and handling it ourselves.

At the age of twelve, I thought that my life was crazy, and that no one loved me. I felt unprotected and alone. My grandmother died when I was eight years old, and she was my guardian; with her, I knew that I was covered and loved. She made sure that I was loved and pretty. Just typing this makes me remember all the love that she gave me. I was molested from the age of five until twelve, and I remember I went to summer Bible camp in 1978 and was baptized. The funny thing about that is I gave my life to God for a peanut butter and jelly sandwich. The counselor asked if I knew what it meant to be baptized, and I replied yes. I said that it is an outward show of my inner glow, and that when I went under, all my sins would be washed away. He offered me an extra PB&J sandwich if I would go and be baptized, so I went; God got my soul for cheap, but his price was a greater cost than I can ever repay. After that, I recall a difference in my life and in the way I behaved and responded to people; I was different, and the things I did without getting caught were over. I was exposed in all that I did, and my mother whipped me often—and I mean *often*. After being dipped, it was as if I was worse; I was already bad or crying out for attention and not the negative crap I was given.

Before being baptized, all the things that I was doing seemed OK. I'm saying this because I was being molested by this person that would tell me that I was God's "chosen one." They would say things like that God had called for me to take care of his "special angel," and if I did that, he would have a special place in heaven for me. This person abused me for the longest of any that touched me. I tried to tell, but I was called a liar and then whipped and silenced. The hurt turned into anger, and I become rebellious.

After I was baptized, I changed and did not believe that God sent me to serve this person. I knew that what I had been told all those years had been a lie—a lie to keep me in place. (I was only eight at the time.) The story had been that if I ever told anyone, God himself would kill that person. Again, I was eight, and out of fear, I believed.

My Story

The fear of killing someone if I told kept me silent. My anger became rage, and I was acting out everywhere. I could not tell, so I fought, and I stole, and I hated everybody but my grandmother.

I guess it was the spring of 1979 when my grandmother was holding me and asking, "What's the matter, Carlos?" (She never called me Carla.) I didn't want to tell her, but she promised to always protect me, and that God would fix it all. I told my grandmamma what was going on and all that had been said. I told her why I couldn't tell anyone, because the person had said that whoever I told would die—that God would kill them. My grandmamma told me that God was a god of love and not of hate, and that he would not do that. She told me how much God loved me, and that she was proud of me for telling. She reminded me that, because I gave my life to him, he would always be there for me.

It wasn't long after I told my grandmother that she went into the hospital and never came out. This was June of 1979; my protector died. They said that it was her heart—something about a bypass for her heart. Now, in my eight-year-old mind, I killed her. I had put too much on her heart, and it had stopped up, and I had killed her. My abuser had been right that God would kill anyone I told. I did it to my grandmother, and I could never tell anyone else or they would die too because of me. My grandmother's death silenced the abused child in me and closed the door to my trust in people and, especially, God. After her death, the abuse continued, and it was worse and more often.

Many know that family secrets are easily kept, but when the tongues of the hurt turn the lock of the door of those secrets, the lives of all the people are changed. Why is it that when people get angry at others, they want to hurt those who are innocent in the picture? They take the most fragile of all and shatter them for their own private victories. At this point in my life, I wondered why I did not look like my sisters and brother, and why I was the different one. I was different in so many ways. I believed the stories that my brother told me; he said that his mama had found me in the alley behind the trash can, and that she had felt sorry for me and took me in. That made it easy for me to not connect, and I did not want to be there with her who I called mother. Let me explain: my mother told me that when I was two weeks old, I had a very high fever that would not come down. She took me to the hospital, and they dipped me in rubbing alcohol to bring it down, and when they brought me back up, all of my hair burned off and my skin wrinkled to the point that I looked like an old man. My mother said they could never figure out what spiked my fever, but when my grandmother saw me, her response was, "She is so ugly that only a grandmother could love her." So most of my time was spent with my grandmother. She was my protector; she was my mother.

It was fall of 1982, and the tongue of the wicked was in my ear. The locks of the secret door began to turn. My aunt was angry at my mother for whatever reason, I don't know. Well, she decided to tell me that my father was not my father, and that my mother was a liar and a cheat, and that she had never wanted me, but had had me in hopes that someone would love her more. Wow—to me, it was a slap into the hurt I was already feeling. To me, it's one thing to feel something and not know it for a fact, but when the feeling of fiction becomes facts, the dimensions of life shift to become your reality.

Ol' folks say, "Get the boots out, 'cause the *@!# has hit the fan." I felt like I got slapped in the face. Let's see how it's smelling: first, the sexual abuse was happening again; second, I was black, and I was ugly, stupid, and hurting; and third, I was alone, with no grandmother to protect me, and a God that I was not sure of. It smells bad to me even just remembering it.

I was struggling with all of this, and it seems as if my life was blank. There was no purpose to this little girl other than pleasing others, at the cost of dying every time. My mother was straining in how to deal with me. She thought that whippings all the time was the key, to beat me into the perfect child that she wanted, until I was no longer there. (For those reading this book, please be mindful of the words you speak over, to, and in a child's life. Words will form them more greatly than you will ever image.) I got worse, and I got to the point that I wouldn't even cry: total shutdown. I got lost inside my idea of life, and that's where I stayed. Although I had major grief with God, I still went to church. My mother never made me go; I went on my own. It was the place I looked for my grandmother; it was the last place I saw her.

By the spring, it was worse. I was lost, and it was as if no one cared if I was there or not. The abuse was at the point of being bad—*really* bad—and no one believed me. It was to the point that another would beat me with a sock of soap. They would put the soap in the sock and beat me. They said that it wouldn't leave a mark, and the reason was because I was the favorite now. I was the favorite, "more special," and it wasn't fair. I remember that they said, "I love you, and I want you to be special to me too. It's not fair that God trains his head angels in his own time. You have advanced, and it's not fair." All I thought was, "What the hell!" and "Why me!" The line that was said to me was, "If you give me this, I'll give you that, and it's how we love each other." Damn! This is not a good experience to have as a little girl.

My Story

I was tired and the only thing my mind was chirping was, "Go find grandmamma; go be with the one that protected you best. Go; she is waiting to help you and to take you out again. GO!" Well, the only way was through death. My mother had lots of medicine in the cabinet; I chose pills because it was painless. A knife would be messy (at that time I was a cutter to ease the pain), and a gun would be loud, and people would ask too many questions. So the pills were easy, and I had great access to them. I remember they were sleeping pills and painkillers, just what I needed: sleep that would kill the pain.

It was early spring, because it was still cold. I remember walking to the bus stop and going into a housing complex breezeway sitting down to go to sleep. I often did this to wait for the bus, staying out of the cold. My bus driver would never get off the bus to come and get me; he would just pull up as if he was taking off, and I would come running out. This morning was different; I didn't come running out, so he got off the bus and came in and got me. (Thank you!) I can remember bits and pieces of what happened next; he got me on the bus and sat me in the first seat. He asked, "What the hell's wrong with you, girl?" and I said, "I'm sleepy, and I want to see my grandmother." Next, I remember him shaking me to wake me up, and him crying and saying "God, no!" then lights flashing and voices saying,

"No, she can't die, she's too young. She's a baby! What did she take? Lord, not her." And then the black came.

Two days later, I woke up in the mental ward at Mercy Hospital in Chicago. I was crying and wondering what had happened. Was I too stupid to even get this right? Then the voice said to me, "Let her die, because I have let you live. Let her die." The voice was referring to the twelve-year-old girl that came to die, not the one he had let live: me. I said no, and I plugged her up on life support because I was the only one that could take care of her, and I wasn't about to let God. Now I believe that had I let her go then, my life would have had a different twist. But it was not until March 2012 that I unplugged her and let her go in peace. It took me thirty years to stop looking back and taking care of the dead thing in my life.

STEP 1

Unplug

To disconnect from the power source, to be free of an obstruction, and to unclog is what "unplug" means, and it is the *first step*. The *first step* to the road of true freedom in the glory of the Lord, without a pause of thought. Psalm 51:6 says, "Behold, thou desirest truth in the inward parts: and in the hidden part thou shalt make me to know wisdom." He wants those things that you keep hidden from the world, the things that you have suppressed down so deep that they are even hidden from yourself.

This passage of Scripture comes from King David's sin with Bathsheba and the murder of her husband, all for his lust. What he did was throw the rock and hide his hand. Who would tell the king that he was wrong, or challenge his authority? Who would do such a thing? This is how we feel also after doing a dirty deed and seeing no one else around to speak of the crime; we hide our hands too. Jeremiah 23:24 reminds us of the omnipresence of God: "Can any hide himself in secret places that I shall not see him? saith the LORD. Do not I fill the heaven and earth? saith the LORD." Just like King David, we hide the truth and believe the lie, but God, who is everywhere, sees all things, and takes our wrongs by bringing them to the light.

God sent his prophet to the king, and the prophet Nathan was wise in his approach. He painted a picture for the king to see, to view from the outside while looking in. Seeing the faults in others is easy when we ourselves are living in our own lies. So David viewed the picture and passed a harsh judgement on it. He called for death in what he saw outwardly, never giving thought to what he had hidden in his inward parts.

When you're inward *parts* meet the hidden *part*—well, let's say it this way: when your lies meet God's truth, wisdom is the gain. King David had his deed tucked deep within himself. He believed that it was a well-kept deed; because of his authority, no one would speak of it, nor would they every call him out on it. But the call of God was on his life, and he wasn't just representing himself; David is known as a man after God's own heart. The hidden deeds will come out in order that God's name will stay righteous. So David had to come clean before the Lord. He had to cry out from a pure place so that the acts of his sins would be forgiven and the life of his child would be spared. The wages of sin is death; David's first child with Bathsheba died, and David's heart was cleared before the Lord. David gained wisdom that nothing is hidden from the Lord our God.

The Lord knew that when I was twelve, I didn't let the little girl die. He knew then that I had trust issues with him, and he watched me as I plugged her up to the life-support system.

At twelve, I thought I was slick and that I could outsmart God. Just like David, I didn't understand the omnipresence of God. So for years I pretended that God would never see me go back and check on the little girl, and depend on the strength of her pain to carry me through the next thirty years of my life. I would escape back to her when life was being cruel to me, and I would remember her and what she did to survive. I used her hurts to justify my wrongs, bad behaviors, and dumb choices. I knew that God sent people (prophets) to speak into my life to let it go, but I would go through the motion with them, just as she would have for the people to leave us alone. Sometimes I would do what I called a "spiritual hop." I would simply shift in a spiritual movement, and if the person could catch or see what I was doing, I wouldn't play with them because I knew they were real and from God. Even after knowing that, it still took me thirty years, tons of hurts, three marriages, and the loss of children and of a parent to finally unplug her.

It was Saturday, March 17, 2012 at 2:30 a.m. when God spoke clearly to me. I was preparing to speak at a conference, and I had no idea what I was going to say. The theme was birthing, and the scripture was Psalm 51:6. That morning, God began to speak so clearly, and he made his voice a visual clarity, meaning that I could see all that he spoke of.

He said, "I have so much in you, but you can't deliver! You are holding on to things that I have already released and moved beyond, but I can't get it out of you because you won't let her die. She is the little girl who has been dead to me so many years now, the one who suffered so many hurts, and who thought she was alone. The little girl was tired when she came to me, and I accepted her then, but you are the one I let live. You are the one who I need to live to tell her story, but you plugged her up to keep her alive as your crutch. You did it for two reasons: one, because you didn't trust me completely, and two, because you were afraid of what was next for you." I can remember weeping, because it was all true. Then he said, "*Unplug!* Unplug her and live according to the designed plan that I have set for your life. *Unplug* her so that I can birth the greatness I put inside you. CL Sharkey, I called you, and I knew you before time. And now I want to share *you*, not the abused, hurt, untrusting, angry, conning little girl, but the woman that will be birthed today. Let her die that you may live."

On the third Saturday of March 2012, I told the story, and I went back and *unplugged* the little girl. I apologized to her, and I told her that she would be OK with him and that I was so sorry for keeping her away from grandmamma for so long. I asked her to please forgive me and to go.

Unplugging is hard, but it is necessary. For years I thought I was never good enough for anyone, and that everything that I loved would be taken from me, but it was because I held on to a weight that kept me bound in its own insecurities. Today, unplug from all that's a weight on you, so that you too shall live and not die, and to declare the works of the Lord.

Before going ahead, let's pray.

Father, in the name of Jesus, thank you for forgiving us of all our sins and our iniquities. Father, thank you for allowing your truth to meet my lies, and for opening my eyes to your omnipresence around me. Now, Lord, as I unplug from my past hurts, failures, rejections, insecurities, and lack of trust in you, I pray that you will lead me, guide me, and redeem my soul, as your Word promises. And Lord, I am ready to meet my new self in you and through you. In Jesus' name, Amen.

Step 2

Not Comparing Yourself

Now that we have unplugged from yesterday, the next step is rather difficult. How do I move forward? Who am I? Where do I go from here? These are the question that will flow through your mind, and they could become a stumbling block to you. We often won't take the next step, because we are not sure of our footing. A poem that I wrote says:

I'm on the edge, and the next thing will push me over.
But don't do it, cause I'm not ready.
I can't go back to the things that put me here
For life to me is more than death itself, and if to die, let it be my reasons why.
No tangle of the bondage of freed freedom can hold me, but the next step will lead me to a place I've never seen.
So how do I do this not knowing if I will land on my feet and start running, or if the wings of his grace will fly me over to the next level, or if I will meet my fate with a crash suddenly to a hash place of my choice and decisions?

Hear my cry, hear my cry. I won't go back, and can't go. My steps slip for the freedom that you guaranteed. To the unknown I go, with hell behind me calling constantly, and a future of self-insecurity, but your grace had taken my place. *Yes, and good-bye*, I must live and not die.

Forward I go, to meet the unknown introduction of anew, *yes, yes, yes* to the truth of your Word.

This poem opens the close of the first chapter. Once we decide to pull the plug, we can let our past die and live in the new creation that he has promised. We stand in a holding pattern.

The children of Israel were brought out of Egypt, but they stayed in a holding pattern by their mindset. The holding pattern was not the place that they were going, because the path was clear even though there was not a map to follow. It was the holding pattern of the blank slate, and their mindset that put a pause on their promise.

Saul was on his way to persecute Christians when he had his Damascus experience. This experience left him in a holding pattern for three days. Becoming blind suddenly will put anyone in a holding pattern.

We are the same way, because when the blood frees us from our yesterday, we become new creatures. 2 Corinthians 5:17 says,

"Therefore if any man be in Christ, he is a new creature: old things are passed away; behold, all things are become new." It's new! Never seen or used, fresh out of the box, untouched, new, free of sin, newborn in the spirit of Christ; New!

An introduction is a formal personal presentation of one person to another or others. This is where the old you meets the new you! It sounds crazy, but picture the oil running down your head and being crowned king, and you had just came in from tending the sheep. The prophet Samuel was sent to Jesse's house to anoint the next king of Israel.

1 Samuel 16:11-13: "And Samuel said unto Jesse, Are here all thy children? And he said, There remaineth yet the youngest, and, behold, he keepeth the sheep. And Samuel said unto Jesse, Send and fetch him: for we will not sit down till he come hither. And he sent, and brought him in. Now he was ruddy, and withal a beautiful countenance, and goodly to look to. And the Lord said, Arise, anoint him: for this is he. Then Samuel took the horn of oil, and anointed him in the midst of his brethren: and the Spirit of the Lord came upon David from that day forward. So Samuel rose up, and went to Ramah."

This is a familiar story, and I can relate to this one; he was called from the field where he was tending the sheep. He was nasty and smelly, and he was unprepared for the thing that was given to him.

He was anointed to be king just a few steps out of a field. He met his future with his past standing front and present. David was not born in the palace, he was not born into high society, and he didn't have any formal training on be a king. He was now in a holding pattern.

This is how I felt for years when people would tell me that much is given and much is required. I didn't understand what this meant, so I was in a holding pattern. I put myself in this holding pattern because of my lack of trust from hurt. So I was in a holding pattern for more than thirty years.

Like the children of Israel, my mindset was plugged to what had just happened to me, to the little girl that I plugged up to life support. Even after I had pulled the plug, I was still in a holding pattern. Like David, I had never been introduced or trained to be the person who I was anointed to be.

Holding patterns can go on for years, and it's like a movie that never ends. There is no closure, because what's next is unknown to you, but God has the master plan for his creation. Part of his plan is for us to hear and obey him, and to not listen to the place that we came from.

I was in a holding pattern for thirty years because I wouldn't let the little girl go. It was as if my past gave me superpowers to do anything, good, bad, or ugly. All this occurred while I was trying to be a new creature. I was out and wandering like the children of Israel, not because of my complaining, but because of my holding on to a dead thing. Like David, I had no training in this new place, and I couldn't identify my teacher, again because of a lack of trust.

The holding pattern is a dangerous place, because it's the old meeting the new, like new paint on an old canvas. This is the place where it feels like hope and the fire of the Lord leaves, and you are blind, in a dark room, looking for the crack of light to exit. Let me encourage myself with Psalm 46:10, "Be still, and know that I am God," or Psalm 34:22, "The LORD redeemeth the soul of his servants: and none of them that trust in him shall be desolate." OK, I'm breathing now, and I'm ready to hit the landing strip. As the plane lands, the excitement of nerves and uncertainties come, but I'm ready.

"Therefore if any man be in Christ, he is a new creature: old things are passed away; behold, all things are become new" (2 Corinthians 5:17). This is the scripture that I held on to in the landing time. I'm new, I'm new, and it wasn't until I came out of the "duh" stage that I grasped the idea that I was a *new creature!*

This was a dangerous place, because I began to compare myself against others and the old me. I compared myself to people who were going where I was going or who were there already. I wanted to sound like this person or that one. I wanted to hoop and draw the crowd in, and they would love whenever I spoke and would fall out. Then if I needed money, they would give it without any questions asked. My mind had forgot that I was a *new creature*! How could I tell, because I went back to hustling for what I wanted, like a ventriloquist doll or a dummy sitting on the lap of depending on me and what I knew to get it, Trusting in God is the game changer!

So I was trying to do the old me in the new sight. I was trying to be like everyone I saw on television, or waiting on others to tell me that I did a great job. I wanted to be told that I was doing a great job in whatever I did, from dancing to mothering, to even being a wife. I wanted someone to validate me in all that I did. I wanted that approval in order to know that I was doing it right this time.

I was in a *crisis identity*! That's right, not an "identity crisis," but a "crisis identity," because I was a new creature (identity), but I didn't know what to do (crisis). I knew that by accepting Christ, I was a new creature; the old things were passed away, and I was new. What that meant to me was I could no longer operate in the old systems that I had unplugged from—system down. It was like waking from a long coma and learning to live all over again. Like a baby, I was looking for the pattern of a path that I could mock up my life after.

To find me and come out of this crisis, I had to go to the creator of the creature. So to the Bible I went. The first thing I read was 2

Corinthians 10:12, "For we dare not make ourselves of the number, or compare ourselves with some that commend themselves: but they measuring themselves by themselves, and comparing themselves among themselves, are not wise." What God is saying is that you won't see yourself in them because he has designed you after himself, and when you look for yourself in man, you will never find the designed plan of your life, because they are not God. At this point, I was scared and ready to turn around, but I couldn't. I needed to know what I looked like, who I looked like, and what my purpose was. These are the questions that kept me moving and searching the Word for answers.

What I did next was take baby steps before the big step in the next chapter. The baby steps I took all involved the Word because I had to read the manual to understand the product or to see the vision that the creator had for the creature.

- **Tiptoe 1**—2 Timothy 2:15: The only one I needed to prove myself to was God. (This scripture will eliminate what others think of you.)
- **Tiptoe 2**—Psalm 46:10: Be still and know. You can make it happen, but waiting on God to tell you "when" will keep you on course with fewer detours

- **Tiptoe 3**—Galatians 6:9: Don't give up; we are almost there! (This verse is a pep talk to yourself.) This scripture keeps me moving, because I got to see his finished product in me. But the process—OMG!

- **Tiptoe 4**—Psalm 34:22: Trust; this one wasn't all a bed of roses and easy steps. I stumbled and fell, but here God would remind me to get up and trust him.

- **Tiptoe 5**—Psalm 91:11: I'm not alone. He sent his angels to have charge over me and to lead me and to follow his commands as long as I was in the will of God.

- **Tiptoe 6**—Psalm 51:3–6: "For I acknowledge my transgressions: and my sin is ever before me. Against thee, and thee only, have sinned, and done this evil in thy sight: that thou mightiest be justified when thou speakest, and be clear when thou judgest. Behold, I was shapen in iniquity; and in sin did my mother conceive me. Behold, thou direst truth in the inward parts: and in the hidden part thou shalt make me to know wisdom."

First I needed to admit that I ignored the voice of God and did what I wanted. I realized that I only hurt God and what he had planned for me.

Then I crept to facts of my past, and these steps allowed me to creep into the emotional bondage of my past, and to release the hurt of the pain that was caused to myself through the pain of others. Crisis identity means to stop living in the hurt of other's pain. It's often been said that hurting people hurt people; misery loves company. This is where the buck *stops*! I came out of the stuff that they gave me, the stuff I allowed to take place and kept silent about. I was going along with their pain as if it was mine. My emotional bondage came because I took what happened to them and called it mine. People will give you what they have and make you believe it or have you live like it's yours from the beginning.

Now I could see myself, because I was comparing my pain to their hurt. I took on their form and image, and it changed my identity and took me into crisis. Be careful not to take up others' hurt and live with it as your pain. I'm saying this because I did everything I could to heal their hurt, but I lost myself trying to give them the love that they needed to be healed and to move forward. I left myself standing in abuse, not seeing that I was dying. The crisis is that your identity is gone to them.

After unplugging from my past and asking the creator for my design, I asked, "What do I look like to him?" and he took me on a journey of *single steps* to paint on the new canvas the vision of his marvelous work. I found out that I have my own color palette, bright and vibrant and full of life. When I first saw it, I was scared because I had never seen such beauty in myself. I always saw it in other and was able to recognize it in them, but never in myself. I finally discovered that I could never see in others what's not in me. I had to learn how to see past my own past. *I am fearfully and wonderfully made!* I see and am seeing *me* one step at a time.

I think of King David; he was anointed king three times, and he had to run for half of that time just to stay alive. He didn't know how to be a king, but something on the inside of him knew what he was. King Saul once put his armor on David to make him a great warrior. The Bible tells us that David declared that this armor was too big for him, and that he had all he needed to fight. Trying to fight the giant in the king's armor, David would never have won the fight, but he remembered the lion and the bear that the true God gave him power to defeat. This story told me that at one point in life, I *did* know the power in me, and we just stop hanging out. Unlike David, who turned down the king's armor, I put it on and tried to fight in it. In the battle, I lost myself trying to please the people. *But no more!* This *step* introduced me to me and connected me to him (the creator). *Note to self:* board meeting in the morning. All members must *attend*! *Me, myself, and I*, along with the creator! Do this to "seek ye first the kingdom of God" that I will never lose: focus on the creator's design for my life.

Before the next *step*, let us pray.

Lord, I thank you for taking the scales off my eyes. Father, thank you for forgiving me and creating the right spirit in me, and for renewing my mind to see you more clearly. Father, all that I am is by your design and your plan. I release all that has come against me and hurt me. I pray that they will be loosed from their past. Now, God, give me peace and continued focus on your purpose for my life as we meet at our board meetings. Thank you. Thank you for showing me all of the colors that you have revealed to me. Lord, thank you for the new canvas, and for continuing to teach me to be a good steward of your gifts. In Jesus' name, Amen!

Time to *step*!

Step 3

Love Responding to Love

I have discovered a great mystery in the Word of God. I have tied Psalm 51:6 to Mark 12:30 as to why love should and does respond to love.

Psalm 51:6: "Behold, thou desirest truth in the inward parts; and in the hidden part thou shalt make me to know wisdom."

Mark 12:30: "And thou shalt love the Lord thy God with all of thy heart, and with all thy soul, and with all thy mind, and with all thy strength: this is the first commandment."

These scriptures are linked to the process of being whole in Christ, that the purpose that is hidden in you will come forth. Again, the Word of God is strategic, pointing to the promises and mysteries of his glory, because he is faithful. Job 12:22 says, "He discovereth deep things out of darkness, and bringeth out to light the shadow of death." Psalm 139:15 says, "My substance was not hid from thee, when I was made in secret, and curiously wrought in the lowest parts of the earth." And Jeremiah 33:3 says, "Call unto me, and I will answer thee, and show thee great and mighty things, which thou knowest not."

Your hidden parts are developed daily. There are two roads that we can travel: *world* and *Christ*. We are in this world, but not of it. So these two roads are very present in our daily walk. Proverbs says, "Train up a child in the way he should go: and when he is old; he will not depart from it" (22:6). This speaks even now, and we can see how without it, the world has the road greatest traveled. This is a principle, and we should constantly teach it to every generation: that the next will be greater than the last. Teaching the Word of God is a must, because without it, the generations will do what pleases their flesh, and not the things of God.

No matter how bad I was as a child, I stayed in church. My grandmother took me to church all the time, and told me stories out of the Bible. She would say to me, "Carlos, sometimes people will love you, and sometimes they won't. Just remember that the Lord's love will last always; he is your shepherd."

When we are introduced to sugar at an early age, we seek that sweet thing to entertain our taste buds. So, if we can start with the Word of God and teach the reverence and respect of Christ as early as possible, we will see the road to salvation more worn at the beginning to end.

In my journey, God has given me four *R*'s to understand how love responds to love works. Each one deals with a part of what I had to surrender to him *every day*; this is the daily *renewal*. I'll start at the core, the *heart*; the heart is *repentance*. The Bible tells me that the heart is wicked, so in order for me to come clean, I had to start there.

REPENTANCE

Repentance means deep sorrow, contrition, or regret for any past action. Before I could hear God clearly, I had to search my heart and remember what I had done. Psalm 51:1–12 spoke to me, because it said what I was thinking and feeling. It was against God and only Him that I had sinned. I had done evil in his sight. I hurt the people around me, but really it wasn't them who I hurt; they felt the physical and mental portion, and some scars were left, but the true hurt and pain was to God. After reading, studying, searching out, and asking for help from the Father, my heart became heavy, and the things that I had hidden in my heart became so real that I felt like I wanted to die because of the pain that I had caused for my selfish gain, and because of the pain of what had happened to me.

"The sacrifices of God are a broken spirit: a broken and a contrite heart, O God, thou will not despise" (Psalm 51:17). When I got there, I was tired and ready to die. I wanted the pain to end, but it wasn't the pain caused by others; it was what *I* had done and was still doing to myself. When you are the cheerleader for everyone else, you try to pay your way out of the hurt hiding in your heart, or even just ignore all the symptoms of pain. Empty, alone, and hungry, I had nothing to grab on to in myself because I did not trust me. I was alone because I didn't want to be with myself, and I was hungry, wanting to eat, but was full of @#!%. I couldn't take in any good, but I knew that it was needed to heal me. I didn't want to live, but I was too stubborn to die, and I had no clue that trusting my flesh was the virus that kept me standing still. Finally, one day Psalm 51 started speaking to me. At first I was just repeating what it was saying, crying, and asking God to forgive me for all the hurt that I had done and was doing. At this point, I felt so bad that I couldn't accept his love and forgiveness. I thought myself unworthy.

At first I was just repeating the verses and crying; then, all of a sudden, I stopped crying and started singing that "God had cleaned my heart and had given me a new me." I remember that day every day because my heavy heart was lighter; he gave me a new one. That was the moment that my repentant heart responded to his forgiveness. The Word of God became a living word in me, and I became aware of his forgiveness and his hand that would guide me. Even until this day, God has forgiven me and has taught me to forgive myself. I accepted his love and forgiveness. I *accepted*!

He had renewed the right spirit in me, and he was upholding me with his free spirit; he restored the joy of my salvation, and he did not cast me away from his presence. He did not take his Holy Spirit from me, but he created a *new creature* in me, starting with my heart. To release my heart allows him to hold what he created as beautiful, even today. This step was long and steep, and it's something I still do every day. The struggle is real! *It does not happen overnight. Please don't give up on the first day.*

REDEEMED SOUL

The next *R* is *redeemed*, and it deals with the soul. My heart is the core, and now the *soul* is where the gift lies. First, to *redeem* means to buy back, exchange, or recover. Listen when I read that definition; this word made me realize that something had been removed, but I didn't know what.

OK, since I cleaned my heart, I figured I would ask God what had been lost.

One morning in prayer, I went to the beginning: Genesis. Genesis 2:7 says, "And the LORD God formed man of the dust of the ground, and breathed into his nostrils the breath of life: and man became a living soul." A gift is something given and something received. When it's given, there is a giver and a receiver. In this case, God is the giver, man is the receiver, and the breath of life is the gift. Out of that, man was created, the only creation that was made in the image and likeness of God (Genesis 1: 26–27). The breath of life was the gift given to man, which set him apart from the other creations. God created man in his image and his likeness; that to me means I look like him and think like him. My desires are the same as the creator's, and I can talk like him. (Whatever he spoke came to pass.) These are the benefits to the gifts of being created, the gift of the breath of life, which makes us a living soul to serve a living God.

When I thought about being redeemed, I had to know what I'd lost, because it means "recover" and "buy back." So I went back to the beginning; this is the key for love responding to love. Go back to the beginning of any hurt to see what happened at the starting point. It doesn't matter what the hurt or the pain is. If we go back to the beginning, we can heal by dealing with what was lost at the start.

When I was a kid, I was really bad—yes, *really* bad. But no matter how rough I was or how much trouble I would get into, I was always in church. It was like I was looking for something that I had lost there. I went looking for my grandmamma after her death, because that's the last place I had seen her. So I went back to church to find her.

Adam had a great thing in the garden with God. He walked in the cool of the day with God. They met daily, they talked, they trusted each other, they were company one to another, and they had an understanding of obeisance. This is love responding to love, the creator teaching the creature how to love and how to give it back. Beautiful!

Now sin comes in, and it disconnected the needy from the source. In the garden, the water supply was cut off, and you did it, even though everyone in the matter passed the blame and never realized that it was their reaction that became their action. I think of myself here; when I was in my sin and was disobedient to God and my mother, I lost connection to the thing that I needed. I didn't know how to get back to it, so I would go back to the last place I had it.

I would spend the next forty years trying to reconnect to the gift inside me. This step is so important, because it allowed me to empty out all and become ready to be redeemed. We think being redeemed is automatic, but no, you must be ready, tired, and empty. Christ will accept us with stuff, but the stuff isn't in control. It's just there with a temptation to come back to it.

Redemption says you are worthy and God wants you back. I started reading and seeking the Word of God because I had to get back to the beginning. I talked to him, and he responded through his Word and through other people who had been healed in the same areas as myself. The more I spoke to him, the more he would speak back to me. He began to teach and train me, as if I was back in the garden. God will teach you how to come back to him; he will show that the *cross paid the cost* so that I could come back and be with him again. Love responding to love is possible through the redeeming power of the cross. As I let him in more and more, he conditioned me back to that place of obedience in my heart to love him. By doing this, he went back to the beginning in me; he went back to my soul. It was never my flesh that he wanted, it was my soul. The soul is the connecting point of his love. Even God goes back to the beginning to redeem.

The flesh is a filthy rag that houses our precious soul, and that the breath of God that gives life.

It was the flesh that got judgement and that was kicked out of the garden. The flesh will remind you of all that it likes so that the soul will not get fed. The cross of Calvary has redeemed my soul so I can walk in the cool of the day with God. Psalm 34:22 says, "The LORD redeemeth the soul of his servants: and none of them that trust in him shall be desolate." Receive this scripture no matter what you are dealing with while reading this book. Your soul knows that the homestretch is ahead. Rejoice; this is the third step, and freedom is waiting—total *freedom! Don't stop.* My mama would tell me, "A winner never quits, and a quitter will never win." You are on the *won* team—*keep step'n!*

RENEWED MIND

Renew means to revive, to begin, to take up again, or to reestablish. The Bible tells us that we should (revive, begin, reestablish) *renew* our minds every day. Romans 12:2 says, "And be not conformed to this world: but be ye transformed by the renewing of your mind, that ye may prove what is that good, and acceptable, and perfect, will of God." Paul is urging the people to renew their minds because wherever the mind goes, or whatever thoughts the mind thinks, the body will follow with no questions asked.

Renew is where the mind is, and it will find a way to accomplish whatever the mind is on. We are being urged to renew our minds daily because it's the private thoughts of man that become public displays of foolishness. To command my thoughts and gain control of where my steps lead me is the way of God. We have to be able to pull down strongholds that come to sway us off course and shame the name of the Father. I need to make my thoughts fresh daily—no, we need to do it every moment of every day, not just daily, but movement by movement, whatever the mind begins to wander on. If we stay in the moment of the thought, it will become a movement. A single thought can change your view of a matter. We must hear the Apostle Paul; because you are going to think, think on these things: "Whatsoever things are true, whatsoever things are honest, whatsoever things are just, whatsoever things are pure, whatsoever things are lovely, whatsoever things are of good report; if there be any virtue, and if there be any praise, think on these things. Those things, which ye have both learned, and received, and heard, and seen in me, do: and the God of peace shall be with you" (Philippians 4:8–9).

There is a promise that comes when we think on the things that the Apostle Paul spoke of in the above scripture: the God of peace shall be with you. Just by renewing my mind, I get the God of peace; not just the peace, but the God who grants the peace, controls the peace, and establishes the peace. I get him. Having him is worth renewing daily.

REJECT = STRENGTH

This is the last *R* needed to learn how love responds to love. *Reject* means to refuse to take. Refuse to take is equal to "not in my own strength." This is where dealing with my past thinking comes into play, letting me know that I have the ability to do so much, but not it all.

And the Lord God formed man of the dust of the ground—stop! Man comes from dirt, and it is that dirt that houses the breath of life. Imagine you have two cylinders in front of you; both have a closed bottom and an open top. Their shape is circular, and the color is clear. What I see in front of me are two objects, and I believe they are water glasses. That's what I see, and it is possible that they are glasses, but without holding something inside them, they are just cylinders sitting on the table, with a closed bottom and an open top. Man is like this cylinder sitting on the table: an object without a filled purpose. God created us to look like him and to be in his likeness, but we don't take on his form until he blows the breath of life into us. Until the breath, man is a shell needing to be filled—filled with the Spirit of God.

I know some of this sounds kindergarten-ish, but this is how it came for me to see me. In the garden is where sin starts. Adam was disobedient to God's word, and of course he got kicked out. The reason wasn't the woman, but it was that he gave into his fleshly desires. The woman entertained what the serpent said: "Ye shall not surely die.... Ye shall be as gods, knowing good and evil." So she ate and gave it to Adam, and he ate also. The connection died between man and woman and God. How? They became ashamed of what they saw outwardly of themselves, the flesh. After noticing the difference, they sewed fig leaves together to cover themselves, and then hid. Hiding is a guilty admittance. Now, God came to look for his creature and could not find him, so he called out, "Adam, where you are?"

The shame that hid you will be the same shame to reveal you. The flesh will make you hide and believe that no one can see you or even notice the change in you. There's no good thing in the flesh. Galatians 5:19–21 says, "Now the works of the flesh are manifest, which are these; Adultery, fornication, uncleanness, lasciviousness, Idolatry, witchcraft, hatred, variance, emulations, wrath, strife, seditions, heresies, Envyings, murders, drunkenness, revellings, and such like: of the which I tell you before, as I have also told you in time past, that they which do such things shall not inherit the kingdom of God." All of these things are works of the flesh, and they are direct lines of disobedience to the word of God.

I grew up in the city, and had access to all kinds of things. If I wanted to do anything, I knew who, where, when, and how. My mother was strict, and she would beat me down at any time, at any place, with whatever she could get her hands on. (I was bad—*really* bad). So I learned at an early age that I could use my body and get whatever I wanted. Remember, my concept of love was "If you give me this, I'll give you that." As long as I got mine, we were good. Obviously, this was a twisted understanding of this great gift called love. I have done about all of the things listed in the above scripture through my flesh, and it wasn't because I did not know God or even because I didn't go to church; I thought I was making it happen for me with what I had and with how well I could work it. This is why I try not to judge. Because of what I went through as a little child, my mind and my imagination grew with a healthy appetite for more. Mama said, "Curiosity killed the cat, but satisfaction brought him back." Sex was my curiosity; my flesh craved it and had to have it.

Rejection is hard when you like what's rejecting you, and when it fulfills the need of itself. This of all the *R*'s is the hardest for me — that's why it's last. When I let my flesh have its way, I was in control. I was in power, and no one could take what I wasn't giving. Being abused makes you claim your power and authority, and I began to live in a world of "I ain't yo' mess." OK, OK, I became dominant and fearless, letting my flesh lead me. I was the one, the hustler; I was the pimp! As long as my flesh was in demand, not my mind, not my heart, not my soul, my price was up, even in myself. When I realized that I was empty, and that what I was doing in the flesh was not filling something on the inside of me, I had to stop and push all those easy things away. I found myself to be *alone and lonely*.

I was there because when there is no life in you, there is no life in you. It's funny how when you stop giving people your flesh, they stop coming around, and now those who loved you won't even look your way.

People rejected me daily, and they told all that I had done, all that I could do. This part was difficult but doable. The rejection of denying your flesh to your flesh is what will kill you. See, people can be replaced to fulfill the lust of your flesh. Your dance partner can change, and the next may be better, or you can teach them what makes your flesh happy. I have learned that hurt will train others to keep on hurting. Hurt responds to hurt, which makes it easy to keep hurting; it just picks up and tries new pains. You get tired of you, and you want out, but there isn't any place to go. You're stuck with your own flesh, hating it, because you can't find that satisfaction anymore.

It happened suddenly for me; God gave me a choice of *now*. I needed to leave the flesh behind and find me. Let me say it this way: I was empty, and I was full. I was empty because my flesh could not fulfill itself; it always looked outward to pass the blame for its actions. I had only nibbled on Christ, but had never fully sat down to eat at the table that he had spread before me.

My heart went through repentance, my mind was renewed, and my soul was redeemed, but my flesh needed to be rejected. For love to respond to love, obedience becomes the key step to move out from the trees where I was hidden. Just like Adam, I had hidden because of the shame of what I had done in my flesh. The other parts of me had been renewed so that I could seek the word of God. I wanted to begin to walk in the cool of the day with him again, but I had to reject my flesh.

Galatians 5:24–25 says, "And they that are Christ's have crucified the flesh with the affections and lusts. If we live in the Spirit, let us also walk in the Spirit." The scripture says, "have crucified the flesh with the affections and lust." This one got me, because I thought it was telling me to keep on doing what I loved to do in the flesh. This didn't settle right in me, so as God says, "If any of you lack wisdom, let him ask of God." I did, and I found that the verse means that with the same passion, force, and drive that I had pleased my flesh, I should now pursue Christ now that I was in him, while saying no to my flesh and those things that would keep me separate from him.

It was not an overnight job; some things stopped instantly, while others I'm still battling. Now, with the understanding of Christ's love for me, it gets easier day by day. Crucifying my flesh daily allows me to connect with him and to feel the power of his love in all I do. I allow the Spirit of God to invade my flesh and to have total control, so that he will be glorified in the Earth. I need to explain that it is a daily job; I rebuke my flesh minute by minute in a day's time. Paul said, "For the good that I would I do not: but the evil which I would not, that I do" (Romans 7:19).

When I was kicking it with the enemy, my life had some problems. It was nothing major, but when I started denying the enemy access to me, hell came a-looking. Please hear me when I tell you that when you reject this flesh, be ready for the quilt trip that you will take yourself on. Beware that you will become your own worst enemy, but Romans 12:2 tells us, "And be not conformed to this world: but be ye transformed by the renewing of your mind, that ye may prove what is that good, and acceptable, and perfect, will of God." I shouted it down before, and I start declaring and decreeing that I will crucify this flesh, and the angels that the Lord has given charge over me shall fight every mental, emotional, spiritual, physical, and financial battle that the wicked one will bring to me.

Lord, grant me the peace that surpasses all understanding. Grant that your hand will be upon me, and as I acknowledge you in all my ways, give salvation to me in this hour. Lord, as I reject my flesh and bring it unto subjection to Christ Jesus, lead me in all truth according to your will. Please accept this sacrifice, and respond continually with your love. In Jesus' name I pray, Amen.

STEP 4

Whyfacome?

"Wisdom is the principal thing; therefore get wisdom: and with all thy getting get understanding." Proverbs 4:7

I went through all kinds of thing, and I didn't understand why and how this great God that we call on, who is so much in love with and cares for his people, would let these things happen. I was healed but yet bound in a place called *whyfacome*.

I know that will be considered bad English to some, but this step will make sense when you get here. *Whyfacome* is the place where I was healed. I still didn't have an understanding as to why. I know, I was told never to question God, but excuse me, he is my friend and he has called me his friend, I have a right to ask him, *"Whyfacome?"*

This word comes for my now sixteen-year-old daughter when she was about three-ish. It was late, and I was trying to watch a movie I had rented, but I was tired and was only half watching it. Now, she was tucked in her bed, and I thought she was sleep. Then, to my surprise, I got slapped in the face, and she was screaming, "Mommy, *whyfacome, whyfacome* did Jesus make him bad on my eyes?" I couldn't explain it to her the *whyfacome*. So when a thing baffles me, it becomes a *whyfacome*. Getting to this point in my steps, the things that had happened to me baffled me and made me wonder. I didn't have a reason or idea as to why at this point; I screamed, "*Whyfacome?*" to God, and wanted an answer.

I believe that God wants us to have understanding in all the events of life, and to gain wisdom from them. In all thy getting . . .

I then begin to search Scripture to hear God's answer, starting with Romans 8:18: "For I reckon that the sufferings of this present time are not worthy to be compared with the glory which shall be revealed in us." So I thought that though I suffer now, we all come out better. I thought that was crazy, but then I flipped in my Bible to Matthew 27:32–36, the story of the crucifixion of Christ. After reading the story, I cried, but I was still not satisfied, so I studied more. The next scripture was Ephesians 1:11, "In whom also we have obtained an inheritance, being predestined according to the purpose of him who worketh all things after the counsel of his own will." After reading this one, my attitude changed, and I saw that he has always had a plan for my life. And he promised never to put more on me that I can bear. Again that was not enough!

One night in a dream, I saw the garden of Gethsemane, where Jesus was praying that God would do it another way by passing this cup, but he rose and said, "Nevertheless." Jesus knew what he had to go through and why he had to. Without him going to the cross, we would not have life—and have a more *abundant* life—because of his death.

He knew all and yet he went, and if God would have stopped that, then where would I be today? My answer was that God could not come down and save or stop all the things I went through, because he had others coming behind me whose pain would be touched by my healing so that healing would begin in their lives. All things work together for good, and God will give us all we can handle at the appointed time.

I have understanding that my pain has a purpose, the purpose of the power of healing and allowing his glory to be revealed. This unveiled truth allows me to become visible to the Father for use in the worship department.

He took me through to heal me, all because he "seeketh such to worship him" (John 4:23). Now that I will not lie to me, nor to those around me, he can use me in the fullness of his power. My *whyfacome* has turned into worship because I got understanding!

Prayer . . . *Thank you, Father, for giving me the chance to come clean before you and to have a renewed spirit in me. Thank you for giving me strength to move forward and to serve you with all of me, not withholding anything from you but opening up to the Holy Spirit's guidance to live whole and healed in all areas of my life. Thank you for forgiving me, and for restoring and teaching me how to forgive those who have hurt me, abandoned me, and have forgotten me. Thank you, because now, I can serve you with a pure heart. I worship you and give you the total praise. In Jesus' name, Amen.*

- **Step One—Unplugged:** I'm no longer connected to the past things that I used to empower myself.
- **Step Two—No Comparing:** I'm not connected to it anymore, and I will not compare my new house to that old one, thankful for the upgrade! I'm not living in the new while walking in the old.
- **Step Three—Love Responding to Love:** "My soul shall make her boast in the Lord" (Psalm 34:2a). His second wind comes into me by the cross of Jesus Christ.
- **Step Four—Whyfacome?** I gained understanding that his glory is in me, and now my purpose is revealed.

Now it's time to get up!

STEP 5

Rise

Well, we are ready to take the last step. This is a celebrating place, even while being a scary one, because it's time to get up and . . . *live*! *Rise* is the final step in reaching the landing that completes this flight of stairs. Now it is time for me to step in the place that God has designed for me. The steps are calling me to the King's table. I was all disconnected at one point and another because of sin, but the King has requested my presence at his table.

2 Samuel 9 gives us the account of a king's kid disconnected from his stuff. One day, King David wanted to know if there was anyone left from the house of Saul that he might show kindness to for Jonathan's sake. There was one, Jonathan's son Mephibosheth. He had been lame of the feet as a child, they told him. (It's funny how people will always tell your crippling story.)

2 Samuel 9:6-8: "Now when Mephibosheth, the son of Jonathan, the son of Saul, was come unto David, he fell on his face, and did reverence. And David said, Mephibosheth. And he answered, Behold thy servant! And David said unto him, Fear not: for I will surely shew thee kindness for Jonathan thy father's sake, and will restore thee all the land of Saul thy father; and thou shalt eat bread at my table

continually. And he bowed himself, and said, What is thy servant, that thou shouldest look upon such a dead dog as I am?"

Mephibosheth refers to himself as a dead dog; I can relate to this, because he doesn't see what the king sees. I was the same way, not being able to see or hear anything good about myself because of where I was, and then being lame at the feet. I was in the presence of the King, but was not able to see that the Master empowers me. What he said about himself was what I said to myself when the King called me. I can remember falling down and worshipping him because I was in the presence of the King, presenting my gift that he'd called for. All the things that had done and all who I had hurt by my silly reactions to being hurt; which were my actions. I'd passed the blame to others, and had never thought that the King would one day look for me. I'd never thought that he would want to show kindness to someone like me. Verse 8 is what I felt like—a dead dog—but the King wanted me. People, God had never taken his eye off of you, and now he is calling us to the King's table to eat continually.

The King was extending an invitation to me, and I needed to accept or decline—and who says no to the King? When I accepted and went, my heart was full, and the King was not concerned. He had already forgiven me and healed my heart. The sign for this was that I now stand in front of the King, and I see myself as he sees me.

Through his eyes, I can see the pureness of the love he has for me, and it allows me to see and to operate in the way I look in his eyes. For me to rise, my opinion of myself changed. I stopped letting my past speak, and I shifted my steps. I stopped rehashing what they had said over my life, and I corrected my speech about myself as well. There are no dead dogs here because he has come to give life, and life more abundantly. Surrendering to Christ allowed me to lift up my head and seek him, to be in his image and likeness on a daily basis.

Then He began to give me the things of my Father's house. God showed me here that we are never lost to the things of our Father's house; they're just disconnected and hidden for our safety. For our safety, he allows us to be hidden in a place called Lo-debar, a place without, a "having nothing" place. It really is a diversion for the enemy; he will put us there to hear, heal, and to become humble. Lo-debar is a place of nothing to the natural eye, but to God, it's the place to find *next*: the next one that he can show his kindness, his mercy, and his glory to. It's funny that God shows his glory to the people in this place, and they have to respect you. They thought you had nothing, but you are the King's kid. At the story's start, my opinion of myself was low to nonexistent. I was put in a place that took all my possibilities and turned them into anger. As I'm writing, I have moments where I don't believe that he has chosen me. My opinion of myself was that of others', and I had to step out of their views of me and find and believe my own. Mephibosheth compared himself to a dead dog, and wanted to know why the king would want him. Through understanding this step, I got up out of the hurt of others' opinions.

Romans 12:1, I beseech you therefore, brethren, by the mercies of God, that ye present your bodies a living sacrifice, holy, acceptable unto God, which is your reasonable service.

All of the steps got me to this verse. I crucified my flesh, changed my thoughts, accepted his love, and I will tell of his goodness to all. But what is my reasonable service?

Reasonable means capable of rational behavior or decisions. Service means an act of helpful activity; help; aid. What I had to do was put the definitions together to understand what it meant and how to apply the understanding to my steps.

Reasonable service means being capable of rational behavior or the decision to act helpfully in all activities. It was telling me to think in a better frame of mind that my actions would be helpful in aiding someone else walk with Christ. It's better said as becoming God's witness in the earth. I could no longer operate the way I did in the world. Changing my thoughts also changed my actions, so that I could go back to his original design. "And God said, Let us make

Rise

man in our image, after our likeness: and let them have dominion over the fish of the sea, and over the fowl of the air, and over the cattle, and over all the earth, and over every creeping thing that creepeth upon the earth" (Genesis 1:26).

It's funny that the serpent told woman that if she ate of the tree, she would not die, but that they would become gods. She didn't understand that she was already a god.

She was a god because God said, "Let us make man in our image, after our likeness." This is the plan that he had for us, to look like him so that when he would look from heaven, he would see himself in the earth. He would see the family that he sorry desires in the earth. Adam walked with God in the cool of the day; he had total communication with the Father, and they had a bond. This bond would allow them to trust each other, and to not question or doubt the love between them, but to fully operate and live in wholeness of love — love responding to love. He enjoys seeing himself in the earth, just like when we have children, we want to see which side of the family is seen in the child. We can't wait for the baby to begin to form its features and traits so that we can see the love of the parents expressed in the earth. Well, God is the same way; he wants and so desire for us to be in his image. He waits for us to grow in him, to be formed in the image that he had in his mind from the first day that he said, "Let us." It is his design that he looks for.

It was his likeness that developed my features so that I would begin to look more and more like him. I found his likeness—or his attributes—in Galatians 5:22–23: "But the fruit of the Spirit is love, joy, peace, longsuffering, gentleness, goodness, faith, Meekness, temperance: against such there is no law." It was crazy that I had done most of the things listed in Galatians 5:19–21, and did them with no second thought. The flesh doesn't care as long as it is satisfied; the false evidence appears to be real. There was an afterthought of guilt and shame, and I explained earlier that shame will expose you.

Then I needed more to fill the void that I had; but I had to look back to where I'd lost it. Back to the beginning! The beginning is the breath that was given to man to make us into the image and likeness of God. Galatians 5 tells what the Spirit has and what it offers, and it explains plainly the benefits of walking in the likeness of God.

What is the likeness of God? What did I need to see within me that was his? Now, these questions are set up to only have one answer, and if we read Galatians 5:22 correctly, *love* is the answer!

Love is the likeness that is in you that makes us in his likeness. It is his love that corrects, embraces, changes, and starts anew. 1 Corinthians 13:1–2 says, "Though I speak with the tongues of men and of angels, and have not charity, I am become as sounding brass, or a tinkling cymbal. And though I have the gift of prophecy, and understand all mysteries, and all knowledge; and though I have all faith, so that I could remove mountains, and have not charity, I am nothing." This scripture tells me I can do great exploits in life, but not have love in me; then, I am nothing.

This is the part of the journey in which I had to become the first partaker of my own fruit. In this, I have told how I had to let things of my past go, to unplug, to work through my crisis identity. Releasing and rejecting all these, I found myself. But to see me in the likeness of God, I had to forgive me and then begin to love me. Not others, not family, not my ex-husbands, but me!

When I dealt with *rise*, I couldn't get up totally without me, myself, and I all intact and on the same team, and the only way I did was through self-forgiveness. I believe that if Adam had admitted that he'd failed instead of passing the blame back to the woman that God had given him, or if woman had admitted to listening to the serpent, childbirth would be easier naturally. The garden would still be in existence today. And just maybe, if they could have simply admitted to their portion in the event and asked for forgiveness of the Father, they would have been able to forgive themselves also. Repentance is the key factor here, not just to God for the act of disobedience, but for the knowledge of the wrongdoing, for not yielding to the Holy Spirit, and then for blaming others for what I caused myself. Until I did this, I questioned my own judgement of all things, things like the new people that came into my life, my spending habits, or just trusting myself to take care of me. Let me explain; one Sunday, my pastor preached on not breaking rank. He told about how in the solider formation, the solider behind you has got your back, so you are to fight forward without looking back. I was crying out to God and saying, "But I never broke rank. I still pray for those who left me and destroyed me, and I have forgiven them and I love them. So why am I on the altar?" This is what I was saying to God. Then he responded to me, "Yes, you have cut down your tree of hurt, but you didn't dig up the stump of the tree, so the roots are still in the ground. And because of that, you can't love freely. You can't respond to my love totally because you are still rooted in looking back." WOW, what a divine revelation. I then began to cry, "Dig it up! I need your help; I don't want anything to produce from those roots." Well, God did help me to dig it all up, and after we were finished, it left a huge, enormous hole. I was empty and needed to be filled. Then I saw his love go in, and joy, peace, longsuffering (patience), gentleness, goodness, faith, meekness, and temperance. They kept coming until the hole was filled, and he packed it down and handed me two keys to the kingdom. The first was forgiveness, and the other was self-forgiveness. So now when my past would look at me, it would now see *him*. Even when I look at me, I see him.

I can *rise* in the likeness of him, all because on this journey he taught me how to love me like he loves me, and in loving me like he does, I can love others. This is my reasonable service.

My prayer for you is that you find yourself through the cluster of unpacked boxes locked in your mind, and that you can dig up the roots of anything that bears the fruit of your yesterday. I pray that true love in the likeness of God finds you taking *single steps* as he sends his love to cover you, and that you will respond back to him by accepting and giving it all back to him.

Father, thank you that this book has found the one you wrote it for, and that through it I now see me as you see me, and that my love is truly responding to you with love. In Jesus' name, Amen.